WHEN

the

BEE

STINGS

RAQUEL FRANCO

**THOUGHT
CATALOG**
Books

THOUGHTCATALOG.COM
NEW YORK · LOS ANGELES

**THOUGHT
CATALOG**
Books

Published by Thought Catalog Books, an
imprint of the digital magazine Thought
Catalog, which is owned and operated
by The Thought & Expression Company
LLC, an independent media organiza-
tion based in Brooklyn, New York and
Los Angeles, California.

This book was produced by Chris Lavergne
and Noelle Beams with art direction and
design by KJ Parish. Special thanks to
Bianca Sparacino for creative editorial
direction and Isidoros Karamitopoulos for
circulation management.

Visit us online at thoughtcatalog.com and
shopcatalog.com.

Made in the United States of America.

ISBN 978-1-949759-32-7

ACKNOWLEDGEMENT

Thank you to the poetry community for always lending a helping hand, whether it be editing or reading my drafts. I wouldn't be where I am today without you.

To girlfriends who hold your hair back, spill the tea, and make sure you don't do anything stupid without them. We are stronger together. Help your sisters and give eachother grace.

To Thought Catalog for giving me the opportunity to present this collection to you in the most beautiful way. It has been a dream come true.

To my babies, Gabriel and Penelope, who saved me.

To God, for without Him I would be nothing.

To you, dear reader, you are not alone in this world. It is an honor to have you here with me. Thank you for your support.

The bee does
more
than sting.
She builds.

WISHING

on

PETER PAN

BOYS

I know your spine is carrying
cracked mason jar memories
of a boy who handed out promises
like penny wishes in the fountain
at the park,
told you to just have faith
and trust and a little bit of pixie dust
but wishing on Peter Pan boys
isn't worth your neck
hung heavy,
isn't worth the loss
of your crown,
so unfold your shoulders
and set all your ideas of Neverland
on fire.

BURN

These men,
they fear your tongue.
Want to slap a label
over your mouth

and call you mad.
They fear your bonfire.
Ready to use their own body
of water to watch you drown.

Resist.

Keep shouting, ferocious throat.
Keep swimming, shark bite.
Keep fueling, tinder ready.
Burn. Burn. Burn. Burn.

WHEN I WEAR RED LIPSTICK

I line my mouth in beeswax, oil
courage. Press my lips together,
lit up like *The Big Apple*
painted in red.

He tells me I look like an exit
sign, doesn't like when I wear
lipstick but I never asked
for his opinion.

I am all prowess, Cupid's bow,
poison-tipped, aiming for
his pearly white teeth.
When I wear red lipstick

the temperature of my bravery
rises. I am tea kettle boil,
confident like a man dressed
in a pinstripe suit. My mouth

reminding me of all the power
a woman can possess, a smooth
criminal.

It is a brave thing
to allow your heart to love
after someone has carved
out a piece and left
you jagged.

ALL THE STUPID THINGS I CONSIDERED AFTER THE BREAKUP

1. Sleeping. Forever. Letting the carousel of the sun and moon travel on without me.

2. Buying a treadmill to shrink my sad body into something he'd beg to have back.

3. Writing poems where every syllable was dripping in his name. *(Wait, I did do that.)*

4. Dying. Maybe by driving full speed on the highway until I crashed into a concrete museum for broken hearts.

5. Texting him. Showing up at his door. Stopping by his work. Going on a walk in the park where we used to steal kisses under the cherry blossom branches, anything to see his creamy, brown sugar skin again.

6. Dedicating my book to him, the one I spent
   two years writing and bleeding my own saltwater
   blood for.

7. Hating myself. Feeling like I was a plane
   ticket he never intended to keep, a destination
   he never intended on staying at.

8. Never letting my glass empty of Chardonnay, just
   swirling and filling, swirling and filling.

9. Calling the local radio station and dedicating Taylor
   Swift's "Lover" to his soft mouth.

10. Writing on his Facebook page: I am the woman you are
    going to regret. I deserve all the promises, all the honey,
    all the tulips, all the open doors, and every last bite.
    Your absence does not make me any less goddess.
    I will not be gutted by your absence.
    (Instead I kept this to myself but remembered every word.)

SATIATES

If you show up at his house
and the only thing you find at the table
are crumbs spilled from his mouth,
know that this is not love.
Love offers you every seat,
a home cooked meal,
bites from each other's spoons.
Love is the thing that satiates.

GHOSTS

My daughter whispers
with her wide, chestnut eyes,
"The ghosts are coming."
She tells me we have to hide,

frantically pulling blankets
over our heads. Beneath the quilted canopy
I discover that all the ghosts
are boys. She means daddy,

her brother, the cat… but I feel myself
thinking, *Sweet girl, oh, how many times*
you will be haunted by those ghosts.
I wish I could place a force field

around her like Jean Grey
but that is not a promise I can fulfill
and my heart knows these hauntings
will eventually give her steel wings

but until then I will let her know that I am here.
I will lend her my arms, collect her tears
in a mason jar and dance away what we can.
I will remind her how worthy and magical
she is and that those ghosts won't haunt forever.

Women are savage, simmering
fever, where flicker turns to blaze,
creeping up the staircase
until the whole house is on fire.
They expect us to stay poised,
coiled into patient women,
but know this:
the ones who truly love you
will know when you need the ocean
and when you need
another match.

You will learn
to live without them,
to resurrect walls
among the empty spaces,
build corridors from the dust
of your broken bones,
recreate home
with your own two hands.

HEARTBREAK SURVIVAL GUIDE

Lay on your shins
with your most honest heart
pressed to the cool bathroom floor
and pray.

Do not vanish in the broken,
in the empty space
on the other side of the bed,
but get lost in something new.

Leave the phone unanswered.
Let him only meet the ring, the busy signal.
Let the floor consume you for only a moment.
Embrace the rug, the carpet, the hardwood floor.

And your heart beating like a faucet drip?
Find gratitude for its perseverance.
Find an open door–the pen, the sun, a friend, a lyric,
a paperback novel, salted caramel

ice cream, grease-slicked French fries,
whatever you need to make
yourself feel warm for a moment.
Learn to marvel at yourself

and revel in your own company
and one day, instead of taking tears
with you into the shower,
take a new appreciation for your resilience.

Love is staying
between life's punch
and life's embrace.
Love is staying
between all the sour
and all the honey.
Love is staying.

IF YOU ARE READING THIS
WITH A HOLLOW HEART,

red-stained rims from a freshly salted wound...
I see you.

I know loneliness.
I have stared up at the popcorn ceiling
in the dead of night with eyes so wilted
and my throat so torn from loss
there was no room for sleep.
I've begged the Lord to take the shattering,
take the scent of cologne from my pillow
(or let it stay forever),
asked why, asked when.

You are not alone
and your prayers won't go unanswered.
The answer will be time,
gentle time.

To be rejected
is not disaster
but the pointing
of the right direction.

FORGETTING

There will be a forgetting.
His name rolling on your tongue.
That aching want as you
busy yourself, pretending not to be
willing the phone to speak. That sticky,
sweet smell he wore after mapping out
your body. The way he ordered his coffee
with a splash of cream, no sugar. His favorite
bourbon and the way it lingered
in your mouth after a kiss. The touch of
his hands, the place you wanted to
live forever. You will forget these things
and the ones you don't won't mean
a damn thing like they used to.

If the boy takes
a piece of you
that you did not offer,
he does not take ownership.
It is always yours
no matter what wounds
he may leave behind.

SIX TEXTS I'M NOT SENDING YOU
after Trista Mateer

1. I let you break me because I'd never felt
so wanted lying underneath your chest,
tangled in your legs, devoured by your mouth.

2. I'd never tell anyone else this
but the truth is…
I'd let you break me again.

3. Another truth. I wish it never broke,
that we had stayed whole and you'd placed all the excuses
in a soda bottle and set them out to sea.

4. I wish I had never met you
but there is no me
without knowing you.

5. I don't know why I loved you so damn much
when I never allowed myself
to be untamed around you.

6. Although there is a graveyard
in my chest with only your tombstone,
I'm better off without you.

I know I am worth
fighting for
but you keep showing up
to the ring
without gloves.
Your white flags
are never surrender
just careless goodbyes
but that doesn't make me
any less punch,
any less applause,
any less trophy.

GROWL

I am used to facing
lions and tigers and wolves
dressed in sheep's clothing.
I may just be a woman to you
but I can bare teeth too.

WOMEN LIKE HUNTING WITCHES TOO

after Taylor Swift's 'Mad Woman'

Men have been dancing
with devils for years,
conjuring spells on women
who were just looking
to be loved. Men have been
masters of manipulation
and been called magicians
but a woman with a sleight
of hand is branded wicked,
burned at the stake. Women,
I say, let's replace fire
with ovation. Take up torches
and go hunting magicians.
Call ourselves audacious.
Call ourselves wild.
Call ourselves a mystery
that isn't theirs to solve.

His mouth is not a window.
It is only shatter.
He has shown you his teeth
and you keep craving the bite.
Girl, you are the entire view,
a balcony with lilac air.
Stop crawling toward
the thing that devours.

RUSSIAN ROULETTE

Sometimes
we let the boy
play Russian roulette.
Our drumming hearts
bloody in their palms.
Shotgun mouth
at the tip
of their tongue.
Convinced we are
bulletproof
we let them palm
our barrel throats
but if you turn love
into a game
there is always a chance
you will get played.

WHEN THEY OFFER YOU LOVE

Make sure their palms are stretched
all the way open.
Arms ready to meet you
on the other side of the bed
and tuck you in like the moon does the sun.
Make sure they have room
for pouring coffee at first blush,
just the way you like it.
Room for lips on your forehead
before you leave to meet the day.
Room to ask for what you need.
Promises to hand out and let you keep.
When they offer you love
make sure it is pomegranate ripe,
soft enough to sink your teeth into.

If you happen to sink
into arms you thought
would hold you,
it's ok.
Your body is weightless.
Like oil on water
you will stay above the surface.

WALK AWAY

He was just an ex-
hale. Just a letting-go.
Just heavy
weight. A fight you won
by being the one
to walk away.

Loving you
was just
a paper dream.
By the end
I was more scar
than girl
but time turns scars
into wings,
paper
into planes,
crooked memories
into parables,
a brand-new version
of the person
you once loved.

WE ARE

not

BAD GIRLS

GIRL IS

Girl is a honey chaser, always buzzing,
taking up space with ease.
Girl is a spotless peach not yet ripened,
one they'll be eager to bruise.
Girl is a river running toward a sea salted body,
tears that come from fresh scars.
Girl is a caterpillar body, fighting for wings,
transforming into something fierce.
Girl is a siren tongue that will one day be heard
from miles, a thunderclap followed by
applause.

Girls, link arms.
Get into trouble
but don't waste it
on boys.
Spend your growing
with each other.
Those boys don't have
enough heart inside their wrists
to hold you yet.

HUNTERS

They call us
hunted girls
but we are the hunters,
raised into assassins.
Smoke screen
mouths
dressed in red
lipstick.
Our skin,
trapdoors.
Our tongues,
a weapon.

CHILDHOOD

We were the sewer street
kings and queens. Grocery store
hunters. Sidewalk maps guiding
us through a childhood summer
dream. Boy crush wanderers trying to
discover names for uncharted
feelings. If only we could've held
on to those days a little longer,
stretched those cherub hours and
stayed mud pie dirty and unbothered
by anything outside our holy
make-believe domain.

SUNDAY SERVICE
for Jessica

Like the seats of a rundown church pew
you are all my childhood memories
tied together by the bitterness
we held for our mothers
and how much we both wished
on mosaic stained glass windows
for our mothers to love us better.
You have always been
my most trusted confessional.
Your purest heart holding
my secrets like a tight-lipped priest.
Never the judge. Never the jury.
Just a shoulder for tears

and the aroma of brownies
that you made for me
wafting from your oven
and from the kitchen
we'd always arrive on the front porch
where the wooden swing
was our alter. Where we shared
Virginia Slims and our fears
of getting older and never having
the roots of our dreams meet the sun.
God, I miss those days
when our friendship was like
a Sunday Service, a place
I could always come to,
a place where I could fall
to my knees and spill.

I don't think it's ever been easy, at least not for me.
I could never walk a straight line,
always veered more toward sadness.
I'd met happiness a few times

but joy, joy was some type of sugar
I didn't have the palette for.
My six-year-old belly was full of moth wings
that craved the taste of butterflies.

Walking to school my unripened hands carried
my lemon yellow plastic lunchbox
holding crispy potato chips and
a peanut butter and strawberry jelly sandwich

made by my mother's hands
and along with my blue bookbag
I gave depression a piggyback ride
every day to and from school.

I didn't know why I felt so much,
why I swelled with melancholy.
My mother didn't understand
when I turned sour but didn't believe

in therapy or medication.
One day I found poetry to mute
my ugly emotions, painted the page
to feel more like paperweight and less like

an anchor. I didn't ever want to lose my muse,
avoided the therapist's chair, but words
weren't thick enough to hold me
and I folded into a shape of myself

I did not recognize. Desperate, I broke
the dam of my anguish in a therapist's office
and with one little pill the fog lifted
and I was still me and life was a little

easier, a little more like lunchbox,
jungle gym days and the only thing I wished
was that I grabbed onto helping
hands a little earlier.

FOLKLORE

Let this be
a new tale,
one delicate whisper
to the next.
Tell your daughters
and their daughters
and their daughters
to let their strawberry
wild spill over.
Leave this world
marked by their sharp
tongues
and gentle palms.
Rattle their cages
and demand respect.
Never play the damsel.
Tell them that women are
unforgettable,
spines that hold
hero's stories
that should never
be bridled.

I JUST WANTED TO THANK YOU
for Amber

I hadn't seen him in two weeks,
felt like our love had been a fable.
He came by to tell me it was over.
I can't remember a word he said,
his mouth just kept spilling
a blurred set of words and the only thing
I could comprehend was
that he did not love me.
I begged him to stay but he left
forever. I texted you first.
You came straight from the airport
and laid in bed with me while I drowned
in my own salt and bedsheets.
Stayed until the stars went to sleep
and I could breathe again.

HOW TO SAVE A GIRL

Don't call her beautiful.
Call her a masterpiece.
Let her know
she was not created

to chase love.
He is not the light
and she is not a moth.
She is love

and has been since
the womb.
Let her feel everything.
Let her say she is depressed,

a long-lost version of herself.
Let her say she is afraid
of holding the future
and having it collapse

in her hands.
Let her say she is in love,
flushed and floating
for the first time.

Let her say she is angry,
that life is crooked and unfair.
Let her be whatever
she needs to be.

Don't bottlecap her feelings
but catch her tears and place them
in a glass bottle.
Tell her they are beautiful

and that's where rainbows
are made.
Tell her she has been given
a mouth to say,

'I can. I will. I am.'
Let her know
she was carved
from the Lord's own palms

and given purpose,
given the armor
to survive the punches.
In her back pocket

she carries faith, hope and love.
Warn her that love is tricky.

It will save you and sadly,
it will break you.

It won't be the band aid
to fix every wound.
Sometimes you have to
let it go

but it will make its way
back to you, like the sun
wakes after a storm
and on the days it hides

behind the clouds, make it.
Create love and let it cradle
the ones that need it most.

You and your sister were releasing
a procession of tears in our living room,
trying to live through your brother's
last hours. I was about to leave,

suffocating from the raven of grief
hovering in the air. I had all too recently escaped
the palms of mourning wrapped around
my own throat. "How do you get through it?"

you asked, eyes red rimmed and desperate
for an immaculate solution. My belly ached
for you, watching your fear of goodbye
trickle down your face, fading into the carpet.

I had no answers I could tie up
for you and make them sound sweeter
or easier. Even worse, I was leaving you.
Death's touch was too fresh on my skin.

My mother had only been resting in the earth's
soil six months. This should've been the reason
I stayed. I should've cried rivers with you, held
your arms together to soften the fall. I knew better.

I know that tragedies are made to birth

helping hands but instead of offering hands,
I replied, "You just do."

TO MY YOUNGER SELF

I know every day you grow
more gas-pedal pressed.
You are tired of asking permission,
ready to make your own decisions
but girl, the lazy summer hours
without obligations are your honeycomb
pockets of time. Surrender
to the slow backroads
of your youth. Don't be in such a hurry
to bare your teeth and call
yourself woman.

SAY TO THEM

I look down at my daughter
bent over the table,
her cinnamon-sugar curls falling
in her face and she says, "That hurts."

"What does?"

She lifts her head
and I see teeth marks on her arm
from her own mouth.
"Baby," I say.

"Don't do that.
Be kind to yourself.
Of course that hurts.
You have to be soft,

be gentle with yourself."
She shows me again,
pulls her sleeve
back over her arm.

I realize
we women have a bad habit
of hurting ourselves
for a little attention.

This is a ritual that needs
breaking, cracked at the roots.
Needs broken even in our
three-year-old girls.

Say to them:
Be soft, more apricot skin.
Be gentle, more rainwater touch.
Be kind, more praise in your throat.

My finger slid down over the list of names.
Jessica, Lindsay, Beth, Megan…
My name wasn't on the list.
I didn't make the cheerleading squad.
My heart cracked and I stood still.
It was the summer going into seventh grade.
The first thing I had ever worked for,
spent sweat, hours, muscle, belief
and it didn't buy me a damn thing
but my mama, my mama told me
to pray, so I prayed, fervently. Kneeled at my daybed,
hands pressed to God, begging for a miracle,
I prayed through June and the strawberry moon.
I prayed through July and the dog days
of summer and when August came
He answered. One of the girls from the team
suddenly had to move. The spot was mine
to claim. Now this may seem like
a trivial tale about cheerleading
but this was my first tangible evidence
of the truth of God's word,
evidence of what faith could accomplish,
what holding on to hope could achieve.
I grabbed it, placed it in the skin of my palm
and I never let go.

SPILL

Nylon sleeping bags in ballerina pink,
lilac, and candy apple red.
All lined up on the basement floor
with little girl toes tucked inside,

bellies swirling with anticipation
of an uncharted night.
What are they spilling
from such pure and naked tongues,

that have yet to taste a kiss
from a boy that will give them a lesson
in what it means to break open?
What do they spill

when they have yet to discover
what their eyes loathe about their limbs,
what they envy in the body
that lies next to them?

What is there to spill
when no one has yet told them
that the world will make them work
harder for their dreams,

make them feel small,
muzzle their mouths?
What whispers did these girls spill
in the dark while the parents slept upstairs?

What pure words did they dream?

ODE TO THE GIRLS IN THE
NIGHT CLUB BATHROOM

To the tiny, underage girl
with the scared but hopeful, amber eyes
asking me for my drink.
I appreciate your bravery,

your hunger for a taste.
I smile and hand you the sweating bottleneck beer.
Leave feeling grateful you trusted a sister
and not a guy with bad intentions.

To the girl puking broken secrets
into a porcelain bowl.
Cherish that girl holding back your hair,
tracing circles on your spine.

She will help you put your jigsaw parts back together.
To the girl spilling salted cocktails
down her flushed cheeks.
The boy you came here to find,

the one holding a tumbler full
of a good man's forgery,
isn't worth the minutes you stand there
in the corner of the stall.

Take this moment by your fists,
wipe the mascara running and dance
like you are the only one in the room.
And to the girl standing in front of her own reflection,

red mouth whispering, "Mirror, mirror, am I worthy of desire?"
You don't need a thirsty man's approval.
You are a neon light humming, an audacious thing,
a mirror ball that would cause any man to sober.

INSIDE VOICES

As children we are taught
to use our inside voices
but girls who become women
are still told to keep quiet,
not to rise higher than a man's chest,
still treated like toys
and the ones who have lungs
to say what they mean
are just seen as bad girls
who don't follow rules.

WE SHOULD BE ALLIES

Who turned hopscotch
into a game of chess?
Who told little girls
with big dream eyes
that only one of us could
be queen?
Who told them we weren't capable
of breaking glass ceilings
together?
This rivalry has been marked
on our backs
from days when all a woman
could earn was a man.
They gave us claws
and sharp teeth
to turn on one another,
vying for attention,
using our sister's backs
as pawns
but I think it's time
to turn the tables
and when they ask us
to checkmate,
we bare our teeth
and take the knights.

WHEN THE BEE STINGS

It is said a colony of bees
consists of one queen
and up to forty thousand female
worker bees, an orchestra of flapping wings.

If the colony is ever met
with an intruder, maybe a waspy man
with hungry hands,
the worker bees will attack. Divide

and conquer, venom sting.
When the bee stings, with their weapon
they lose their life. Breath for breath
they die for their sisters and their Queen.

They live to protect the colony.
I wonder what more we could do to protect
our sisterhood, a howling pink army
of women standing together, determined

to never let them in without permission.

I KNEW SHE WAS MY BEST FRIEND

when she always let me have the boy.
I knew she was my sister
when she never left me behind,
never hesitated to take my hand.

At an NSYNC concert when Lisa was brought on stage
through a crowd of screaming girls,
she made them bring me along.
She's never judged

my poor decisions even when I swallowed
too many shots of Jager trying to wash
down the depression stuck
in my throat or when I let boys

with slimy hands have my parts.
I remember the year we both bought
the exact same prom dress. I was grounded, forbidden
to go so we avoided looking like doppelgängers.

Once we drove to Philadelphia
to audition for MTV's *The Real World*.
We laughed the whole way, open throat
girlhood giggling at our tasteless jokes

and beef jerky sword fights. Together we had

no shame in acting like kids.
We pranked called and texted boys
long after it was acceptable

but it made people laugh.
One year I left Columbus, the city
that helped mold me from girl to woman.
I could find my way blindfolded

through its streets with my bare hands
but I decided to try on bravery.
Moved to Vegas, a place where
I'd never even tasted the air

and when I couldn't quite catch
my breath in that sin city she flew
out and drove me the 2006 miles
back home without question

or conviction. We're not perfect.
We've hurt each other a time or two
but there's no not forgiving her.
We were fearless in each other's presence.

Our parents were terrified of our wild
but she was the one place I felt free.
Aside from our clothes, we shared
each other's wings and lent each other our spines,

an unspoken understanding
that no one else could comprehend
but us.

A FRIEND

When boys left me for dead,
hit and run on a crowded boulevard
a friend picked me up in a getaway car.

When depression made a home of my brittle body
and boarded up windows,
and anxiety put up a barbed wire fence
so my thoughts couldn't make their way out,
a friend reminded me how the sun
is always the headliner behind the rain's opening act.

When my mom took her place in heaven too early
and the earth no longer felt solid
a friend became a shadow to my grief
to remind me I wasn't alone.

When the roles of a woman:

mother,
daughter,
boss,
wife,
sister,
friend,
human

stack up like poker chips
and no one else understands
the weight of my ante, a friend
is always there to bet on me.

MY GOLDEN-HAIRED KNIGHT

for Mollie

I don't know why that stupid boy
took so much of me
but he left nothing.
A ghost town,
just dust and breeze.
You came and saved me
from my handmade gutted graveyard,
pulled me out of bed,
reintroduced me to fresh air
and forced me to stop hiding from the sun.
Spoke to my frail spirit
and reminded me that I had mountains
to move. You've always been
the warning signal and gentle
push I needed when I walked
too close to despair. You are
my golden-haired knight.
I've never needed a man
when I had a friend like you.

Hold tight to the hands
of women who,
just when you need it,
turn rain into whiskey,
clouds into laughter,
and gray hours
into honey butter.

SMILE

with

ALL YOUR

TEETH

I'm beginning to remember myself.
The skin I've been dressed in,
the bones my past have built.
I'm gaining balance from
clumsily walking through winter.
The fog is clearing
and my spine is unfolding.
My spine is rising back up.

WHAT IS IT YOU CARRY
DOWN TO THE BONE?

Let it be
faith, the belief that anything
you can imagine
can manifest in this world.

Let it be
hope, a never-ending expectation
that hanging on is worth the burn,
is worth thick-skinned hands.

Let it be
love, a technicolor swarm
of selfless open arms
beneath your tender rib cage.

You might fail every day,
scrape your elbows,
dirty your hands,
but you are still conquering.
You are here.
You are showing up
and that, that is the first step
toward achieving.

Like bitter stuck between
your teeth.
Like staring in the bathroom mirror
and seeing nothing
but soft when all you crave is bone.
When the therapist tells you
you are suffering from
severe depression and anxiety
and you may need medication
for the rest of your life
and all you hear is crazy.
I was born crazy.
Feeling like worry is a disease
you can't scrub away
and every person you touch
might catch it.
Like the word "enough"
doesn't apply to you.
Like love may never catch you
and you may spend the rest of your days
crashing into the pavement.
Like you may only ever be seen
as something to look at, to judge, to martyr,
to fear.

Every single day
you are given,
you are able
to take the grapefruit sun
and the milk-drawn moon
into your arms
and declare
that it is yours for
the taking.

Find a way to smile
with all your teeth on display
during these running pages
of time. Let your mouth
gape open and let laughter
pour from your throat
and not let up.

WE ARE ALL JOURNEY

The grass is always
green somewhere,
sunbaked heels sinking in.

Curtains always open,
light never stops
spilling through glass windows.

We all have witnessed
laughter pouring
from our salted mouths.

We are all made
of apple butter days
and memories full
of a thousand charcoal clouds.

We are all journey
and sunset and sunrise
and pulse and breath.
We all are.

I feel as though
all the beautiful words
have poured out of me.
I am dehydrated tongue
and parched letters.
Where did all the poetry go?
When did I wake up
so thirsty?

WHAT I LIVE FOR

Autumn, where the maple leaves go to die and spring,
where my backyard resurrects into magnolia branches.

The peach syrup that runs inside
my children's throats when they say *Mama*.
Their twig arms wrapped around my tree trunk body.

A fresh page and all the possibilities a poem can give.

Songs that put a fever in your pulse.

The break of slippery mango flesh between teeth,
juice running down my fingers.

Bourbon in a shot glass cheering
to the family we made, wild and fearless women.

Love, that has always been the occasion
to show up with your most open arms
no matter how many times it has been shattered.

There won't always be
salt inside your lungs,
tsunamis in your teeth.
Sunshine will find your tongue,
soften all your sharp edges
like honey to meet the healing.

I am not boarded-up
windows, a forgotten home.
There is always a way
to rebuild, to pour into
what was once hollow.

SPARK

When I say,
'Don't let anyone stop you
from living a life set on fire.'
I mean
you need to find the match.
I mean
the fuel, the whiskey, the coals.
I mean
if all you have
are two sticks
then rub them together.
There is no creating a spark
without the first strike.

You are brewing.
A storm at the back of your throat.
Let go. Give your voice lungs.
Let your cup runneth over.
You have every right
to let it rain from your fingertips
and show them how beautiful
you sound.

MY OWN ADVICE

I tell others to be strong.
Wear the red lipstick.
Rebel against their
expectations.
But here I am strolling
beneath streetlamps
with sadness between my toes,
drifting miles from myself.
Feeling as though I wear
the mask of an imposter.
But through the swirling
smoke of doubt I find the words
to tell myself:

I can
I will
I am

just as I would to anyone else.

I KNOW ANXIETY

I know anxiety well.
She has haunted me for years,
preyed upon me at a raw nine years old,
begged me to stay up late with her
and count fears with her like sheep.
She leaves when she wants.
Turns up out of nowhere and brings panic with her.
She is sweat and stomach full of hornet's wings,
my head dizzy like a heavy pendulum.
I've learned to live with her,
take a pill the size of a freckle
to keep her at bay and all those fears
she's flung at me.
I stare them in the face and keep
one foot in front of the other.
I feel the fear on my neck
but I no longer allow it
to imprison my mind.

We are constantly finding
and losing ourselves,
butterflies being spun
back into their cocoons.
Limbs learning new ways
to unfold gracefully
till one day we emerge
with dragon wings.

The venture down
this yellow brick road
is long. Waiting for
open doors,
never knowing when
it will wind or bend.
Some days it is more busy
signal than answer
but there will be days when
a window breaks and grants
you a small victory, a gentle
hushed breeze that confirms
you are headed in the right
direction and that,
that is the hope that carries.

COLORING OUTSIDE
THE LINES

Will you
have the courage
to color
outside the lines?
To call yourself
a rebel and be
authentically you?
Show nothing
but the bare bones
and refuse to cover
them up?
Will you call yourself
more than a dreamer
and choose dream over
comfort?
Refuse to choke
on the word no,
be the thing that determines
your own verdict?

Amongst the tumble of life's
sticks and stones,
protect your cherry blossom smile,
your baby's breath peace,
your juniper laughter,
your magnolia hope.
Protect it. Protect it. Protect it.

RETURN

Some days I feel
like I am carrying
a broken hallelujah
in the back of my throat,
a song I can't quite swallow,
a hope I can't quite catch,
but it always returns
like the prodigal son
and I remember
it always will.

Tell me something girl,
have you given yourself
permission to want,
to take it with bark and bite,
to let your grief simmer
and fuel your fists to persist?
Have you let them see
how your punch has wings,
that no matter how much
you may bleed
you were never built
to meet the ground?

REGENERATION

There will be coming undone,
an unraveling, a shedding
of old skin. Your hours
spent with a torn
stomach of regret,
and sunken promises from
empty mouths
will reveal new pores,
reveal your bark pressed
with vigor.

HOPE WILL BE THE SHELTER

Restless can feel like white-knuckled
fists in the corridors of your belly,
a panicked maze of thoughts
swarming in your mind,
but there is always hope.
Hope will ease the grip
of your worried hands.
Hope will be the shelter,
your holy cave to rest
your weary eyes.
Hope will reach through
the storm and offer
calm.

There is still light undiscovered,
rejoicing that has yet to ripen.
There are still hours to be had,
tangerine days to inhale.

CATCH FIRE

You may feel helpless,
delicate,
like all steel has drained
from your ankles.
You may feel like a ghost
of someone you used to be
but there is tinder in the lining
of your stomach that will
catch fire when the moment
is right. In time you will return
to yourself.

SAY

I am still learning
my own language.
How to say love.
How to say joy.
How to say patience.
My tongue clumsily
tiptoeing on words.

There is beauty
in the slow breath
that comes
from letting go of
the things you've been holding
with clenched fists.

Fear smells like blood,
copper pennies.
When it comes,
wafting up your nose,
open your mouth.
Bite.
That's courage.
Lemon on the tongue.
Swallow
and swallow those fears whole.
That's bravery,
honey dripping down your throat.

NOT TODAY

In a world where the sky
is forced to rain,
the ocean seeks to devour
and the sun begs to shine.
We still have the mouths to say,
'Not today.'

Healing involves
a guttural undoing,
a wreckage of salted tears,
a groan from the hollow places
beneath your bones
and the patience to
let it take its course.

Bitter. The bite on the tongue.
Tastes like meeting the pavement.
Tastes like that hushed moment
before a first step.
Tastes like every tiptoed 'what if'.
Tastes like promises spilt
down the front of your chest.

Sweet. The smooth molasses
at the back of the throat.
Tastes like the peak
of the longest climb.
Tastes like whispered, "I love you"
against the neck.
Tastes like another door open.
Tastes like a vow to always rise.

Life. Drink its bitter. Drink its sweet.
Swallow. Savor. Flourish.

To thrive is to create
new pulses,
to keep finding reasons
for this living.

Blink
and all these simple days
will get carried away
by yawning clouds.
Never stop holding
these daffodil minutes
steady in your open palm.

On the days you exit
your door
with messy hair
and yesterday's tears
left on your skin,
you still hold vigor.
You still carry grit,
even when your heart
is filled with mourning.

SAVOR

Soak in the summer
peach hours.
Pursue all this living,
these gifts of breath,
these pages still turning.

Search for rooftop hymns
and staircase confessions.
Make room for a traffic jam
chorus, a grocery aisle waltz,
a laundry pile trampoline park.

Create this one wild life
into something your mouth
will not forget, a space
you did your best to fill.

WINTER

There will be seasons
where your branches
won't bear leaves
and it feels like
the sky will never grant
you another sunny day,
but you will reach a reckoning.
Don't let your cold days
define you.

When you are more shatter,
breath held like a trap door,
allow yourself to exhale.
Allow grace to knock
easy like a Saturday sunrise
and let it crawl into bed with you.

THINGS THAT ARE LARGE

after Sei Shonagon

Your lungs when you have
something to say.
Cedar bookshelves.
The number of seats
at the dining room table.
Your Jupiter dreams.
Forgiveness in your palms.
The leap when you decide
your heels are ready.
The space in your chest
no matter how many times
it has been hammered.
The belief that your collarbones
can carry cities and still triumph.

KEEP SWIMMING

It may feel like
you are fighting the ocean
but keep swimming.
Be relentless.
The waves will cease,
ease their jabs.
Nothing rages forever.

Sometimes it is as simple
as asking yourself,
what does getting better
look like today?

THANKFUL

No matter how weary
the day,
hold thanks
between
your praying hands
and say Amen.

WHAT TENDERNESS SMELLS LIKE

Lavender, lilac and everything
purple. Eucalyptus rubbed
on my chest by my mother's hands.
Similac on the tongue
of a newborn's breath.
Grandma's fried chicken crackling
in the fryer, red potatoes roasting
in the oven, and sweet greens wilting
in the pot. The harvest of pumpkin,
cinnamon and bonfires in October.
The trace of peppermint oil
from your aftershave
left on my pillow.

HALLELUJAH

Wake up each day
and walk like promise,
like rejoice,
like redemption,
like hallelujah
and say hallelujah.
Hallelujah.

SOME DAYS

Some days
will be more grit.
Less honeysuckle sun.
Less lavender sky.
But we can still find
softness
within our weeping
hours.

I am still learning
balance, when to show
my teeth and when to lead
with tender palms.
What I'm learning
is that balance is mostly
found in staying tender,
in leading with love.

LIVE

Live life to the brim.
Live more barefoot,
more toes on cool grass,
catching neon fireflies.
Live with more arms wide open,
ribs tender enough
to let love in.
Live life with more tree house climbing,
chasing the height of life,
chasing the best views.
Live life filling it up.
Fill it drenched with laughter,
puddle jumping,
talking till strawberry sunrise,
and when it all goes empty...
be determined to fill it again.

We are
all bone
of His bone.
Saved by the
same blood,
a windswept
miracle
made from
the dust.

MY HONEST POEM
after Rudy Francisco

A quarter of the strangers I meet
can't pronounce my name.
Their tongues stumble
over its syllables

but I wouldn't change it
not even for the man
at the end of the aisle.
My name is the only gift

I have from my father
and I don't have the heart
to give it away.
It's Raquel, by the way.

People are unsure of
what they're getting
when they see me.
Like to choose

their own versions.
Black girl, White girl
Hispanic girl but, baby,
I'm all three. Fire in a melting pot,

all boil. Born in June,
they say I am a Gemini.
Though I don't believe
in horoscopes, I find that I am

definitely two sides of a coin.
Both roar and whisper.
I'm quiet at first,
always testing the waters

people wade in,
checking their temperature
and when it's just right
I become a crashing wave,

all honesty and truth.
Some people love
that about me. Some people
can't handle the tide.

Don't like the charcoal taste
my anxiety and depression can leave
on the tongue. I love Jesus
but I don't talk to Him enough.

Dormant guilt sits in my belly
over that truth cause without Him

I'd be nowhere. I'd be no one.
I am a mother of two dragons,

beautiful, fierce things.
I tend to love everything I can't keep,
blinking fireflies, paper napkin poems
and boys with pretty promises.

I give love everything I have.
My time, my money, my skin,
my dignity. The shame used to haunt
me but I evicted those ghosts.

They still knock but I don't let them in.
I enjoy coffee with my cream,
listening to Taylor Swift on repeat
and cuddling of any kind.

There's nothing like the soft,
fireplace warmth of a human
body pressed against your own.
My hobbies include: capturing a genuine smile

in a photograph, collecting books
I may or may not ever read, and forcing words
to reveal as much knowledge and truth
that God has given me to offer.

Sometimes I am just learning
the same lessons over and over
but I am just grateful the pages
keep turning. That God is my publisher

and we're still holding the pen.

WITHOUT PERMISSION

The leaves clap in the wind.
Applaud for nothing.
Applaud just because.
The birds whistle to no one,

need no reason
to make themselves heard.
The ocean settles
and crashes without permission.

As I sit here I realize
I should be more sycamore leaves,
more cardinal wings,
more saltwater.

BUILT

with

BITE

INTO SUGAR

There is no denying this life has teeth.
It will sink past the thick of your flesh,
into your sternum, bone spun
like a pepper grinder. It will disguise itself as
a gift, honey wrapped, bee sting tongue,
but you, you have the power to turn
that pain into flourish and bite back, to turn
those ground bones into sugar.

You are allowed
to defend yourself.
You are worth
defending.
Roar,
but with gentle teeth.

AFTER KHALEESI

I will not be sorry.
You will not find an apology
on my tongue
for my relentless pursuit.
I will not be made small.
I am much more than girl,
than name,
than all the wreckage
I left behind.
My mouth
may have been more fire
but that will not burn my victories,
my dreams, or my faith in me.

I am my own civil war,
a battlefield
I must face alone.

ON HER OWN TERMS

There's this bush outside
my window that on most days
looks like something that needs to be ripped
out by the root and hauled
off to a landfill. My husband threatens
its life every year but I tell him to wait.
Then in the first week of August,
under all that thick raze, she sprouts
her purple petals. I am always fascinated
by her will to bloom on her own terms,
her will to say, "I will flourish
when I am ready."

Be more open throat,
siren tongue.
Do not let fear
strangle your voice.

She is the pin prick
up the back of your arms.
Cocked pistol mouth.
Trigger finger tongue.
She is the bullet.
She is the fire.
To her there is no such thing
as walls that won't crumble,
glass ceilings that won't shatter,
mountains that are too steep.
She is empowered.

When they ask me to smile
I bite their tongues
instead of my own.
I am not resting bitch face.
I am a smile they didn't earn.

I carry oceans
inside my mouth.
Some days I am full,
high tide and saltwater laughter.
On the wrong day
I am violent teeth,
brinier, waves with sharp edges.
Other days I am still. Calm.
Salt kissing the shore.

Do not develop the habit
of devouring yourself
when they try to convince you
you're too much.
You are just enough.

YOU ARE AN ART FORM

Your spilled tears,
your smile ripened like a peach,
your gritted teeth,
your humming fears,
your home sweet home heart.
You are all the perfectly imperfect
sculpted pieces that anyone
would be so lucky to marvel at.

THE BEST DATE YOU'VE HAD IN MONTHS

It's Saturday. Today you choose to spend
your hours wrapped in tenderness
where there is no such thing as lonely,
where sorrow doesn't get a seat at the table.

You take yourself to your favorite bar on High Street,
offer yourself a glass of wine, the buttery liquid
coating your tongue, and you think
this is the best date you've had in months.

At the movies, laughter floats from your throat
between salted bites of greasy popcorn
that you don't have to share with anyone else.
Afterwards you draw yourself a warm bath,

pour lavender Epsom salt and baptize
the water with orange blossom petals and soak
and soak and soak. Pull on an ivory bathrobe,
order takeout and light candles laced with sugar,

gentle arms, and eucalyptus. You go to bed early
where you call both sides of the bed "mine".
Tomorrow you will not ask anyone permission to sleep in,
or to leave the dishes untouched or watch

whatever the hell you want on Netflix all day.
You will bask in your own loving hours
without the company of another taking up space,
because you are more than enough to fill it.

Sometimes the hand
you need to hold
is your own.
The vacancy from
the other side of the bed,
the other side of the phone,
the other side of the dinner table
can only be satiated
by your own company.

YOUR BODY IS POETRY

Your neck, every word
that holds praise.
Your arms, warm teacups.
Your spine, the root
of your conquering.
Your belly, every metaphor
for home.
Your legs, the bittersweet journey,
and your skin, wearing
all the memories
of a beautiful verse.

WEAR BEAUTIFUL

Wear beautiful like you mean it.
Wear beautiful like bare skin.
Wear beautiful like you've never heard otherwise.
Wear beautiful like 'thank you' on your tongue.

Though some days
I am too heavy
to be a warrior.
Too rainwater
to see the sun.
I remain relentless.
I still hold triumph
inside my throat.

NO ONE TELLS YOU

No one tells you
how rage will fill your head
and pour out of your mouth
when the hours have been filled

with screams and reprimands
and Groundhog Day minutes.
No one tells you that guilt
will ride your back

for all the patience you lost
on those tiny souls that you love
more than anything.
They are the last hearts

you'd wish to break,
yet you break them.
Have to step away
before you completely lose

all the wonderful things
you know about them.
Find the softness in your lungs again.
No one tells you

at the end of the day
when all you crave is sweet silence,
failure will cuddle up next to you,
point out all the toys littered on the floor,

the dishes left untouched,
the work you still have left to fit in
and the wine you think you need
but actually does nothing

to curb the shame or the guilt.
No one tells you
it's ok.
You are a good mother.

You are not alone.
Other mothers feel it too.
God gave you these babies
because you were meant to love them

and to show them
what resilience looks like.
So, keeping going mama.
You're doing great.

Lately I am all thorns,
vine on vine,
but I...
I still know
I am snapdragon petals,
a woman,
with beautiful thick skin.

I've been at war with the soft
of my belly since my body grew
roots, began stretching
and adding rings.
I have not been kind
to her. My palms, my eyes
always avoiding her direction
but I will get there. I am working
on raising the white flag, finding
a place for my skin to worship
all her swollen parts. For now, I find
other ways to feel beautiful,
like wearing cherry stem lipstick
or peach garden roses
and baby's breath braided
in my hair. The flush in my cheeks
after a run by the lake. Letting
my spring curls air dry, lay down
my spine. Spilling laughter,
smiling like a confession. Standing
in the light and letting it meet
the arc of my neck, the slope
of my cheekbones. I am a love letter,
no matter the pieces I have yet to admire,
a honey dipped and heavenly thing.

You are not to be made light.
You are a creature of bones
built with vigor, sunlit dragon spine.
Jaws, both psalm and howl.

A CONVERSATION WITH
MY REFLECTION

Today let's set sight
on the beautiful parts
that go unnoticed.
Feast on
the gardenia flower
and mango butter
sleeping in your hair.
Drink on your toasted,
brown sugar skin
that has survived many miles
and stayed soft.
Pull out a seat
for those steaming espresso eyes
that see the world
with a rooftop view.
Say grace for your heart
with that gasoline pulse.
Today let's only feast
on the parts we love.

On the other side
of her broken tongue
is a smile she built
despite all the things
she held so tightly in her throat
and still lost.

A RECIPE FOR LOVING THE
WOMAN IN THE MIRROR

3 drops of lavender oil simmering in the bathtub.

7 hours of sleep beneath just-cleaned sheets.

All the avocados.

Staring at the extra pounds, the stretch marks,
the cellulite, the scars,
and still saying, "This body is something to rejoice."

"No" cocked on the tip of the tongue, ready for all the
boys who try to waste all your sweet hours.

Applause from your own palms
when no one else will offer it up.

Grace like money really does extend itself from trees.

Music and poetry for the gray days
when all the words run out.

Heavy breath, sweat spilled on cheeks,
moving limbs till the heart
and lungs are grateful for air.

Friends, the no bullshit, whiskey in a teacup,
living for the wild
hours kind of friends.

Never ingesting love from clumsy hands or hollow ribs.

Do not diminish
your own value
by uncertainty and disbelief.
You carry love letters
underneath your tongue
and hymns
behind your knees.
You are not
an unworthy creature.

WOMEN'S EVOLUTION

Women are not printed
with expiration dates.
There is no age where
we spoil. We weren't built
for ruin, no rust for time.
We are worth a thousand
words without the picture.
They say men get better
but women get bolder,
unshrink their shoulders,
grow tongues with a knife's edge,
take back their right to declare
themselves a masterpiece
no matter how far the hourglass
has run. We are the ones that keep
getting better through the ages.

You shouldn't carry
your heavy thicket of doubt
like that, let your shoulders
slouch like that. You are
something to see.
Let your spine spill
open and unfold like raze
when you step outside
the front door.

WRIST. HANDS. TEETH.

She may appear delicate,
the soft spot
on the inside of her wrist,
the lavender graze of her hands,
the cherry slick of her mouth…
but don't be fooled.
She was built with bite,
teeth that will sink
if they have to.

IT IS TIME

It is time
we stop waiting
to be told
we are beautiful,
to be told
we are worthy,
to be told
we are magic
in order for us
to believe it to be true.
It was time
the very hour, minute, millisecond
you were born.
It has always been time.
It has *always* been time.

RAQUEL FRANCO is a mixed chick living in Columbus, Ohio. She is the author of two self-published collections, *Keep Me Wild* and *This Woman is Still Girl*. She is also featured in the poetry compilations *Crown Anthology* and *[Dis]Connected Volume 2: Poems & Stories of Connection and Otherwise*. Her work has also been featured in *Harness Magazine, Thought Catalog,* and *Rattle Magazine.*

When she is not committed to the pen she is raising two baby dragons and either dancing, singing, or crying to Taylor Swift.

INSTAGRAM.COM/RAQUELFRANCO.POET